www.sraonline.com

SRA

Printed in the United States of America.

Send all inquiries to:
SRA/McGraw-Hill
4400 Easton Commons
Columbus, OH 43219

Rip and the old man took dinner from the sack. As the other men played, Rip gave them dinner. Then Rip sat down with his dinner. He was so tired that he soon fell asleep.

Rip awoke with the hot sun shining on him. He was not in the clearing, and there were no little men playing long pins. He was back beside the river where he first saw the little old man. "Oh, my. Oh, my," he said. "I've stayed out all night. My wife will be mad, and she'll never believe my story. What will I tell her?"

Rip Van Winkle Part 1

by Washington Irving
retold

Decodable Book Lesson 114

SRA

One sunny afternoon, the little boy decided to have some fun. He cried, "Wolf! Wolf!" as loud as he could. Everyone who could hear him grabbed big sticks and ran to chase away the wolf.

When they found the little boy and the sheep, the little boy was rolling around on the ground laughing. He liked to see all those people leave their work and run to help him.

The next afternoon, the little boy decided to have fun again, so what do you think he did? He cried, "Wolf! Wolf!" as loud as he could. Everyone who could hear him grabbed big sticks and ran to chase away the wolf.

When they found the little boy and the sheep, the little boy was rolling around on the ground laughing. This time the people got mad, and his father hold him, "Lying is not right. One day the wolf will come, and you really will need help, and no one will come to help you." The little boy just laughed.

When everyone was back at the farmer's house, they talked about the little boy and his lying. They decided that someone should teach him a thing or two.

A day or so later, one of the brothers dressed up as a wolf. Then people went out where the boy was watching the sheep. They hid behind a bush to watch.

Once upon a time, there was a little boy who liked to tell lies. Of course, this made people sad.

To help his father, the little boy sometimes watched the sheep. It was his job to keep the wolf away from the sheep. If he saw a wolf, he was to yell as loud as he could, "Wolf! Wolf!" Then anyone who could hear him would help him chase the wolf away.

www.sraonline.com

Printed in the United States of America.

Send all inquiries to:
SRA/McGraw-Hill
4400 Easton Commons
Columbus, OH 43219

The brother who was dressed as a wolf sneaked out from behind the bush and growled. The little boy looked around. His brother dressed as the wolf growled again and walked closer to the little boy and his sheep. The little boy screamed, "Wolf! Wolf! Wolf! Wolf!"

The wolf growled again and got closer and closer. The little boy screamed again, "Wolf! Wolf!" He kept screaming, but no one came to help him.

So the little boy took off running back to the house, all the time telling himself, "I'll never lie again. I'll never lie again." And he didn't.

The Boy Who Cried "Wolf"

by Aesop

Decodable Book Lesson 109

Oh, the tree in a hole
And the hole in the ground
And the green grass grew all around
all around
The green grass grew all around

And on that tree
(And on that tree)
There was a limb
(There was a limb)
The prettiest limb
(The prettiest limb)
That you ever did see
(That you ever did see)

Oh, the limb on the tree
And the tree in a hole
And the hole in the ground
And the green grass grew all around
all around
The green grass grew all around

And on that limb
(And on that limb)
There was a branch
(There was a branch)
The prettiest branch
(The prettiest branch)
That you ever did see
(That you ever did see)

Oh, the branch on the limb
And the limb on the tree
And the tree in a hole
And the hole in the ground
And the green grass grew all around
all around
The green grass grew all around

And on that branch
(And on that branch)
There was a nest
(There was a nest)
The prettiest nest
(The prettiest nest)
That you ever did see
(That you ever did see)

Oh, the nest on the branch
And the branch on the limb
And the limb on the tree
And the tree in a hole
And the hole in the ground
And the green grass grew all around
all around
The green grass grew all around

There was a tree
(There was a tree)
All in the wood
(All in the wood)
The prettiest little tree
(The prettiest little tree)
That you ever did see
(That you ever did see)

The tree in a hole and the hole in the
ground
And the green grass grew all around
all around
And the green grass grew all around

www.sraonline.com

McGraw-Hill SRA

Printed in the United States of America.

Send all inquiries to:
SRA/McGraw-Hill
4400 Easton Commons
Columbus, OH 43219

And in that nest
(And in that nest)
There was an egg
(There was an egg)
The prettiest egg
(The prettiest egg)
That you ever did see
(That you ever did see)

Oh, the egg in the nest
And the nest on the branch
And the branch on the limb
And the limb on the tree
And the tree in a hole
And the hole in the ground
And the green grass grew all around
all around
The green grass grew all around

And in that egg
(And in that egg)
There was a bird
(There was a bird)
The prettiest bird
(The prettiest bird)
That you ever did see
(That you ever did see)

Oh, the bird in the egg
And the egg in the nest
And the nest on the branch
And the branch on the limb
And the limb on the tree
And the tree in a hole
And the hole in the ground
And the green grass grew all around
all around
The green grass grew all around

The Green Grass Grew All Around

folksong

Decodable Book Lesson 104

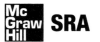

“Run, run as fast as you can. You can’t catch me, I’m the gingerbread man,” he shouted as he ran on.

Soon the gingerbread man ran past farmers working. The farmers saw him and tried to catch him.

“Run, run as fast as you can. You can’t catch me, I’m the gingerbread man. I’ve run away from a little old woman and a little old man, and I’ll run away from you,” he shouted as he ran on.

The gingerbread man ran on till he saw a cow eating grass along the road. The cow saw him and tried to catch him.

“Run, run as fast as you can. You can’t catch me, I’m the gingerbread man. I’ve run away from a little old woman, a little old man, and farmers working, and I’ll run away from you,” he shouted as he ran on.

Not long after that the gingerbread man came upon a fox. The fox saw him. “Run, run as fast as you can. You can’t catch me, I’m the gingerbread man. I’ve run away from a little old woman, a little old man, farmers working, and a cow, and I’ll run away from you,” he shouted as he ran on.

Once upon a time there was a little old man and a little old woman who lived in the woods. One day while the woman baked, she made a gingerbread cake and cut it into the shape of a man. She put frosting on the cake and popped it into the oven.

After a while, she opened the oven door to see how her gingerbread cake was doing. As soon as the oven door was open, the gingerbread man jumped out and ran out the door and down the road. The little old man and the little old woman called after him, but he just kept running.

www.sraonline.com

Printed in the United States of America.

Send all inquiries to:
SRA/McGraw-Hill
4400 Easton Commons
Columbus, OH 43219

Well, the fox had a trick or two. He called out to the gingerbread man, "Run, run as fast as you can. You have run away from a little old woman, a little old man, farmers working, and a cow, but you'll not run away from me. I'm the best runner in the land."

And the fox did catch that gingerbread man and ate him for supper.

The Gingerbread Man

retold
by Moon Rocks
Illustrated by Timothy Pack

Decodable Book Lesson 99

McGraw Hill SRA

When he woke up from his nap, he found that there were no hats in his bag! “Oh, no!” he said to himself and shook his head, “Who took my hats?”

Then he looked up and saw that the tree was full of monkeys with hats on. He yelled at the monkeys. They screamed back. He hopped. They hopped. He tossed a rock at them. They tossed nuts at him.

“Oh, how do I get my hats back?” Ozan asked himself. Upset, he took off his hat and tossed it on the ground. The monkeys tossed their hats also! Ozan did not take any time. He grabbed the hats and went on his way to the next town.

Fifty years later, Habib, grandson of the hat seller Ozan, was walking in the same woods. Habib felt tired and wanted to take a nap in the woods. He found a tree with lots of leaves and cool shade. He put his bag of hats beside him and went to sleep.

5

When Habib woke up, he could not see any of his hats. He started looking for them and found some monkeys sitting in the tree with his hats on. He was upset and did not know what to do. Then he remembered a story his grandfather told him.

Once upon a time there was a hat seller named Ozan. He went from town to town selling hats.

One day, Ozan felt tired and wanted to take a nap in the woods. He found a tree with lots of leaves and cool shade. He put his bag of hats beside himself and went to sleep.

www.sraonline.com

Printed in the United States of America.

Send all inquiries to:
SRA/McGraw-Hill
4400 Easton Commons
Columbus, OH 43219

"Oh, I can trick these monkeys!" said Habib. "I will make them do what I do, and I will get all my hats back!"

Habib waved at the monkeys, and the monkeys waved back at him. He rubbed his head, and the monkeys rubbed their heads. He jumped, and the monkeys jumped. Then, he tossed his hat on the ground.

One monkey jumped down from the tree, walked over to Habib, tapped him on the head and said, "Do you think only you had a grandfather?"

The Hat Seller and the Monkeys

folktale

Decodable Book Lesson 94

SRA

This old man, he played 2,
he played knick knack on my shoe,
With a knick knack, paddy whack,
give the dog a bone;
This old man came rolling home.

This old man, he played 3,
he played knick knack on my knee,
With a knick knack, paddy whack,
give the dog a bone;
This old man came rolling home.

This old man, he played 4,
he played knick knack at my door,
With a knick knack, paddy whack,
give the dog a bone;
This old man came rolling home.

This old man, he played 5,
he played knick knack on a hive,
With a knick knack, paddy whack,
give the dog a bone;
This old man came rolling home.

This old man, he played 6,
he played knick knack with his sticks,
With a knick knack, paddy whack,
give the dog a bone;
This old man came rolling home.

This old man, he played 7,
he played knick knack with his pen,
With a knick knack, paddy whack,
give the dog a bone;
This old man came rolling home.

This old man, he played 1,
he played knick knack with his thumb,
With a knick knack, paddy whack,
give the dog a bone;
This old man came rolling home.

www.sraonline.com

SRA

Printed in the United States of America.

Send all inquiries to:
SRA/McGraw-Hill
4400 Easton Commons
Columbus, OH 43219

This old man, he played 8,
he played knick knack on my gate,
With a knick knack, paddy whack,
give the dog a bone;
This old man came rolling home.

This old man, he played 9,
he played knick knack, rise and shine,
With a knick knack, paddy whack,
give the dog a bone;
This old man came rolling home.

This old man, he played 10,
he played knick knack once again,
With a knick knack, paddy whack,
give the dog a bone;
This old man came rolling home.

This old man

folksong

Decodable Book Lesson 89

McGraw Hill SRA

They met turkey lurkey. henny penny said, “The sky is falling, turkey lurkey.”

“how do you know, henny penny?”

“chicken little told me.”

“how do you know, chicken little?”

“I saw it. I heard it. some of it fell on my tail.”

“We must go and tell the king,” said turkey lurkey.

They met ducky lucky. turkey lurkey said, “The sky is falling, ducky lucky.”

“how do you know, turkey lurkey?”

“henny penny told me.”

“how do you know, henny penny?”

“chicken little told me.”

“how do you know, chicken little?”

“I saw it. I heard it. some of it fell on my tail.”

“We must go and tell the king,” ducky lucky said.

They met goosey loosey. ducky lucky said, “The sky is falling, goosey loosey.”

“how do you know, ducky lucky?”

“Turkey lurkey told me.”

“how do you know, turkey lurkey?”

“henny penny told me.”

“how do you know, henny penny?”

“chicken little told me.”

“how do you know, chicken little?”

“I saw it. I heard it. some of it fell on my tail.”

“We must go and tell the king,” goosey loosey said.

chicken little was in the woods when an acorn fell on his tail. chicken little said, “The sky is falling. I must go and tell the king.”

chicken little met henny penny. chicken little said, “The sky is falling, henny penny.”

henny penny said, “how do you know, chicken little?”

“I saw it. I heard it. some of it fell on my tail.”

“We must go and tell the king,” said henny penny.

www.sraonline.com

Printed in the United States of America.

Send all inquiries to:
SRA/McGraw-Hill
4400 Easton Commons
Columbus, OH 43219

They met foxy loxy. goosey loosey said, "The sky is falling, foxy loxy."

"how do you know, goosey loosey?"

"ducky lucky told me."

"how do you know, ducky lucky?"

"Turkey lurkey told me."

"how do you know, turkey lurkey?"

"henny penny told me."

"how do you know, henny penny?"

"chicken little told me."

"how do you know, chicken little?"

"I saw it. I heard it. some of it fell on my tail."

foxy loxy said, "go into my den, and I will tell the king."

"stop, you silly things," said a rabbit who had been following them. "fox is trying to trick you. let me see your tail, chicken little."

The rabbit reached into chicken little's tail and took out an acorn.

"chicken little, the sky is not falling. this acorn fell from a tree and landed on your tail."

"oh," said chicken little. "Well, let's just go on home and have some dinner." and they did.

chicken little

retold

Decodable Book Lesson 84

McGraw Hill SRA

“now we can find out which is stronger,” said the wind. “let us sēē which of us can māke that man tāke off his cāpe. the one who can do that will be called stronger.”

“that’s what we will do,” said the sun.

sō the wind began to blow. hē puffed and tugged at the man’s cāpe. hē māde rāin bēat the man.

but the colder it got and the mōre it rāined, the tīghter the man held his cāpe around himself. the wind could not get it off.

the sun and the wind wanted to sēē who was stronger. one dāy they saw a man walking down the rōad. hē was wearing a big cāpe.

www.sraonline.com

SRA

Printed in the United States of America.

Send all inquiries to:
SRA/McGraw-Hill
4400 Easton Commons
Columbus, OH 43219

then it was the sun's turn. hē shōne with all his bēams on the man. as it got hotter and hotter, the man ōpened his cāpe. then hē brushed it back. at last hē took it off! the sun was the winner.

the sun and the wind

by Aesop
illustrated by Timothy Pack

Decodable Book Lesson 79

McGraw Hill SRA

when the whēat was rīpe shē said, "who will take this whēat to the mill?"

"not I," said the cat.

"not I," said the duck.

"then I will," said the little red hen, and shē took the whēat to the mill and had it ground into flour.

when shē got the flour hōme shē said, "who will māke bread with this flour?"

"not I," said the cat.

"not I," said the duck.

"then I will," said the little red hen.

when the bread was bāked, shē said, "who will ēat this bread?"

"I will," said the cat.

"I will," said the duck.

the little red hen was in the farm yard with her chicks, when shē found a whēat sēēd.

"who will plant this whēat?" shē said.

"not I," said the cat.

"not I," said the duck.

"then I will," said the little red hen, and shē planted the whēat sēēd.

www.sraonline.com

McGraw-Hill SRA

Printed in the United States of America.

Send all inquiries to:
SRA/McGraw-Hill
4400 Easton Commons
Columbus, OH 43219

"nō, you won't," said the little red hen. "you would not plant the whēat. you would not tāke it to the mill. you would not māke it into bread. so you will not ēat the bread. I will ēat it."

and shē called her chicks to help her.

the little red hen

folk tale

Illustrated by Artifact Group

Decodable Book Lesson 74

McGraw Hill SRA

the other sīde of the
mountain,
the other sīde of the
mountain,
the other sīde of the
mountain,
was all that hē could sēē

was all that hē could sēē,
was all that hē could sēē,
the other sīde of the
mountain,
was all that hē could sēē!

the hōrse went around

ōh, the hōrse went around
with his foot off the
ground.

ōh, the hōrse went around
with his foot off the
ground.

ōh, the hōrse went around
with his foot off the
ground.

ōh, the hōrse went around
with his foot off the
ground.

same song, next verse.

a little bit faster and a little
bit worse.

ōh, the hōrse went around
with his foot off the . . .

ōh, the hōrse went around
with his foot off the . . .

ōh, the hōrse went around
with his foot off the . . .

ōh, the hōrse went around
with his foot off the . . .

the bear went ōver the
mountain

the bear went ōver the
mountain,
the bear went ōver the
mountain,
the bear went ōver the
mountain,
to sēē what hē could sēē

to sēē what hē could sēē,
to sēē what hē could sēē.

www.sraonline.com

SRA

Printed in the United States of America.

Send all inquiries to:
SRA/McGraw-Hill
4400 Easton Commons
Columbus, OH 43219

same song, next verse.

a little bit faster and a little
bit worse.

ōh, the hōrse went around
with his foot off . . .

ōh, the hōrse went around
with his foot off. . .

ōh, the hōrse went around
with his foot off. . .

ōh, the hōrse went around
with his foot off. . .

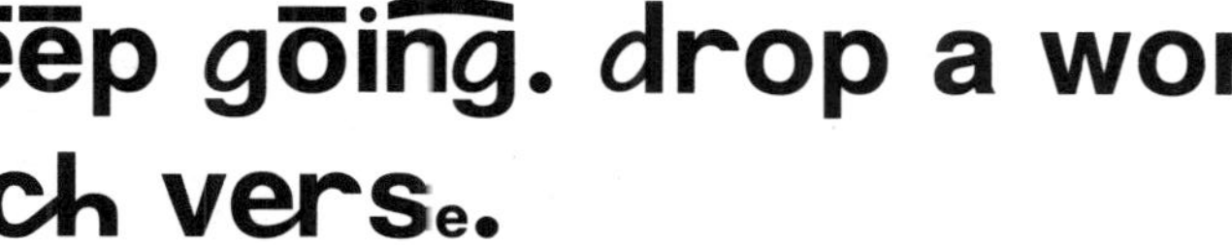

kēēp gōing. drop a word
ēach verse.

silly songs

folk rhymes

Decodable Book Lesson 69

McGraw Hill SRA

there were 8 in a bed and the little one said, “rōll ōver, rōll ōver.”

sō they all rōlled ōver and one fell out.

there were 7 in a bed and the little one said, “rōll ōver, rōll ōver.”

sō they all rōlled ōver and one fell out.

there were 6 in a bed and the little one said, “rōll ōver, rōll ōver.”

sō they all rōlled ōver and one fell out.

there were 5 in a bed and the little one said, “rōll ōver, rōll ōver.”

sō they all rōlled ōver and one fell out.

there were 4 in a bed and the little one said, "rōll ōver, rōll ōver."

sō they all rōlled ōver and one fell out.

there were 3 in a bed and the little one said, "rōll ōver, rōll ōver."

sō they all rōlled ōver and one fell out.

there were 10 in a bed and the little one said, "rōll ōver, rōll ōver."

sō they all rōlled ōver and one fell out.

there were 9 in a bed and the little one said, "rōll ōver, rōll ōver."

sō they all rōlled ōver and one fell out.

www.sraonline.com

SRA

Printed in the United States of America.

Send all inquiries to:
SRA/McGraw-Hill
4400 Easton Commons
Columbus, OH 43219

there were 2 in a bed and the little one said, "rōll ōver, rōll ōver."

sō they all rōlled ōver and one fell out.

there was 1 in the bed and the little one said, "good nīght."

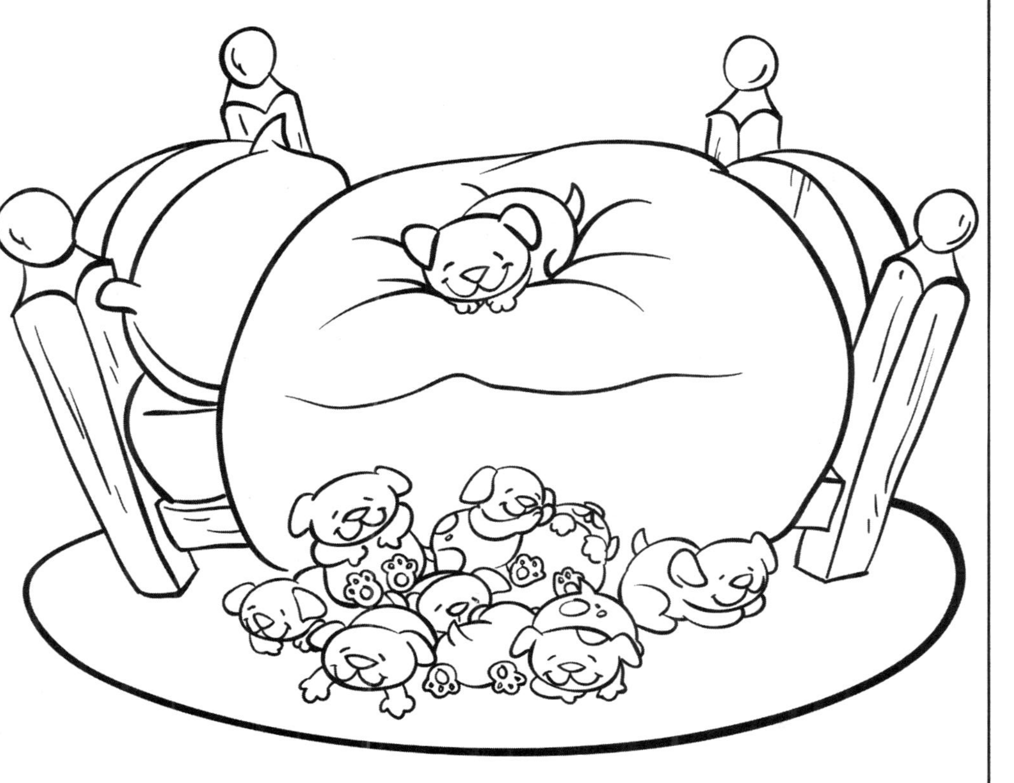

ten in a bed

folk rhyme

Illustrated by Artifact Group

Decodable Book Lesson 64

McGraw Hill SRA

shē'll bē coming around the mountain,

shē'll bē coming around the mountain,

shē'll bē coming around the mountain,

when shē comes,

(when shē comes.)

shē'll bē drīving six whīte hōrses

when shē comes,

(when shē comes.)

shē'll bē drīving six whīte hōrses

when shē comes,

(when shē comes.)

shē'll bē drīving six whīte hōrses,

shē'll bē drīving six whīte hōrses,

shē'll bē drīving six whīte hōrses,

when shē comes,

(when shē comes.)

shē'll bē coming around the mountain

when shē comes,

(when shē comes.)

shē'll bē coming around the mountain

when shē comes,

(when shē comes.)

www.sraonline.com

McGraw-Hill SRA

Printed in the United States of America.

Send all inquiries to:
SRA/McGraw-Hill
4400 Easton Commons
Columbus, OH 43219

ōh, wē'll all gō out to grēēt her

when shē comes,

(when shē comes.)

ōh, wē'll all gō out to grēēt her

when shē comes,

(when shē comes.)

ōh, wē'll all gō out to grēēt her,
ōh, wē'll all gō out to grēēt her,
ōh, wē'll all gō out to grēēt her,
when shē comes,
(when shē comes.)

shē'll bē coming around the mountain

Folksong

Illustrated by Brad Mancuso

Decodable Book Lesson 59

McGraw Hill SRA

the little kittens got down on the ground. they slipped around the hound. the hound smīled in his slēēp. just as the kittens got past the hound, a cow scrēamed, "MOOOOOOOOOOOOOOOO."

the kittens jumped and scrēamed, "OOOOOOOOOOOOOOOOOW."

the hound jumped and scrēamed, "WOOOOOOOOOOOOW."

the cow ran. the kittens ran after the cow. the hound ran after the kittens. they all ran and scrēamed.

"STOP!" shouted the gōat.

bam. bam. bam. the cow stopped. the kittens ran into the cow. the hound ran into the kittens.

"what is gōing on?" asked the gōat.

"the cow scrēamed," said the hound and the kittens. "shē māde us scrēam."

"whȳ did you scrēam, cow?" asked the gōat.

"bēcause I felt līke it. sometīmes I just fēēl līke scrēaming," said the cow.

what is that sound?

the hound is around.

where?

ōver bȳ the barn.

what is he doing?

hē is slēēping.

sh-sh-sh. let's trȳ to slip past him.

www.sraonline.com

Printed in the United States of America.

Send all inquiries to:
SRA/McGraw-Hill
4400 Easton Commons
Columbus, OH 43219

“well, don't scrēam around mē. you silly things, gō awāy.”

sō the cow and the hound and the kitten went back to the barn.

“do you all want to gō for a bīke rīde?” asked the kittens.

“wē can rīde down the rōad and scrēam,” said the cow.

the hound is around

by Walter Ball
Illustrated by Brad Mancuso

Decodable Book Lesson 54

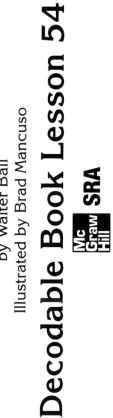

McGraw Hill SRA

sam sat very still. then hē jumped just a little jump.

"stop, sam," ron said. "wē can't jump on the bed."

"just a little, little jump," said sam. "then I'll stop."

sō ron said, "then I'll do just a little jump."

and they did very little jumps on the bed.

then they did not do little jumps. soon they were doing big jumps. and they kept jumping.

jumping. jumping. ōh-h-h-h-h.

STOP!!! yelled jāne. nō more jumping on the bed.

ron and sam stopped.

"bōys. bōys. didn't I sāy, don't jump on the bed?" asked jāne.

"yes," they answered. "but whȳ? jumping on this bed is sō much fun."

"yes, it is," said jāne. "I'll tell you whȳ you shouldn't jump on the bed. bēcause then I want to jump on the bed." Sō jāne jumped on the bed.

ron and sam went to bed. the bedroom was big. there was one big bed. sam sat on the bed. it felt līke a cloud. it felt līke a big pīle of clouds.

"ōh-h-h-h," said sam. "this will bē līke slēēping on a cloud."

"let mē sēē," said ron. ron sat on the bed.

"ōh-h-h-h," said ron. "this will bē līke slēēping on a cloud."

www.sraonline.com

SRA

Printed in the United States of America.

Send all inquiries to:
SRA/McGraw-Hill
4400 Easton Commons
Columbus, OH 43219

"ōh nō, you brōke the bed," sam said. "what will wē do? where will wē slēēp?"

"you will have to slēēp on the flōōr," said jāne. "now I must gō to bed."

sō ron and sam went to slēēp on the bed. and they had a very good slēēp.

not sō good

by Jill Bank

Illustrated by Brad Mancuso

Decodable Book Lesson 49

McGraw Hill SRA

“ōh, sam, it is sō big. what if it can’t sēē us? what if it steps on us?”

a big foot cāme nēar ron. sam yelled, “stop. stop. don’t step on us.”

“what was that,” said the big thing. “I can’t sēē anything. but I can fēēl sōmething with mȳ foot. I must get mȳ glasses.”

the big thing stopped. shē got her glasses sō shē could sēē.

“mȳ, ōh, mȳ,” shē said. “who are you?”

“I am ron,” said the gōat. “and this is sam the duck. who are you?”

“I am jāne. I am an elephant,” jāne answered.

“do you live hēre?” asked ron.

“yes, I live down the rōad. you don’t live hēre. where are you from?” asked jāne.

“wē live on a farm. wē cāme to shop, but it got lāte. the shops are shut,” answered sam.

"I have a big hōme," said jāne. "you could have dinner and stay at mȳ hōme. I would bē happy tō have you."

"thank you sō much," said ron. "it would be good to have dinner and a good slēēp. wē like to slēēp."

sam tōld himself to stop crȳing. sam said, "sam, you and ron are fīne. you will have fun. get back on the cart and gō to the park."

they started fōr the park. then sam saw a big, big thing walking down the rōad. "wow. ron, look. what is that big thing? it has a big nōse and a little tāil. look at that big head. look at thōse ēars. have you ever sēēn anything līke that? wouldn't you love to bē that big?"

www.sraonline.com

McGraw Hill SRA

Printed in the United States of America.

Send all inquiries to:
SRA/McGraw-Hill
4400 Easton Commons
Columbus, OH 43219

sō jāne and sam and ron went dōwn the rōad. when they got to her hōme, jāne said, "let's ēat dinner. then you can slēēp. wē have lots of fun hēre, but there is one thing you can't do."

"what is that?" ron asked.

"you can't jump on the bed. nō jumping on the bed."

"ōh, wē never jump on the bed," said sam.

"never," said ron. "wē never jump on the bed."

jāne's hōme

by Jill Bank
Illustrated by Brad Mancuso

Decodable Book Lesson 44

McGraw Hill SRA

"fastér? if I gō faster you will gō flȳing. you hōld on and don't tell mē to gō faster."

ron walked and walked. sam went to slēēp in his sēat. the cart went slōwer and slōwer. ron stopped in the rōad and dropped his head. ron was slēēping.

at last a big bug bit ron on the ēar. ron jumped and yelled, "what was that? whȳ did you bīte mē, sam? I was having a good drēam."

"I did not bīte you, you silly gōat. you were slēēping. wē will not get to the stōre if you slēēp. now you must run. run to the stōre."

"hōld on you silly duck. if you want mē to run, I will run." ron started running. hē ran faster and faster. ēach tīme hē hit a rock, the cart went up and down. ēach tīme the cart went up and down, sam went up and down.

"stop, ron, stop," sam yelled.

"I can't hēar you," ron answered.

"mȳ tāil, mȳ tāil is sore," sam crīed, and ron ran down the rōad.

sam and the gōat cart started down the rōad. "yes, this is very good," said sam to ron. "don't you think wē will have fun, ron?"

"wē will have fun if you don't trȳ to tell mē what to do," said ron.

"wē are a team, ron. I will not tell you what to do. now gō faster. At this rāte, wē will not get to the stōre in tīme to shop," said sam.

www.sraonline.com

McGraw-Hill SRA

Printed in the United States of America.

Send all inquiries to:
SRA/McGraw-Hill
4400 Easton Commons
Columbus, OH 43219

sam saw the stōre. "wē will bē there soon, ron. you can slōw down now."

ron walked up to the stōre. then sam got down from the cart. hē ran to the stōre and trīed to get in. "oh, nō, nō," said sam. "wē are lāte. wē can't shop."

sam sat down on the steps and crīed, "wē are lāte. it is getting dark. what will wē do?"

"do not crȳ, sam. wē can slēēp in the park. it will bē fun."

down the rōad

by Jill Bank
Illustrated by Brad Mancuso

Decodable Book Lesson 39

McGraw Hill SRA

sam got a big box. “I will help you,” said jill. “I can pāint the box red and yellow. I can pāint your nāme on the box.”

“I must fīnd a sēat fōr the cart,” said sam.

“did you look in the barn?” asked jill. “fīnd a little box and nāil it to the big box.”

“that is good. yes, I will do that,” said sam.

sam got a little box. he sat on it. “this is a hard sēat,” said sam. if I take the cart on the rōad, I will nēēd a pad.”

“I will help you,” said mīles. “I can get a pad fōr the sēat. the pad will be red and the sēat will be yellōw.”

"now I will get the old bikes from the barn. they will be good for the cart," said sam. "then I will get the goat."

"I have to do lots of shopping. the pig and the chicks need feed. mils, the rabbit, must have beans. mack must have bones. jill must have rope, and I need corn," said sam. "I need a ride to the store. I am going to make a goat cart. then I can take the goat cart to the store. A goat cart will hold lots of things."

www.sraonline.com

Printed in the United States of America.

Send all inquiries to:
SRA/McGraw-Hill
4400 Easton Commons
Columbus, OH 43219

"let's gō, ron. let's gō to the stōre," said sam.

sam and the gōat cart

by Jill Bank
Illustrated by Brad Mancuso

Decodable Book Lesson 34

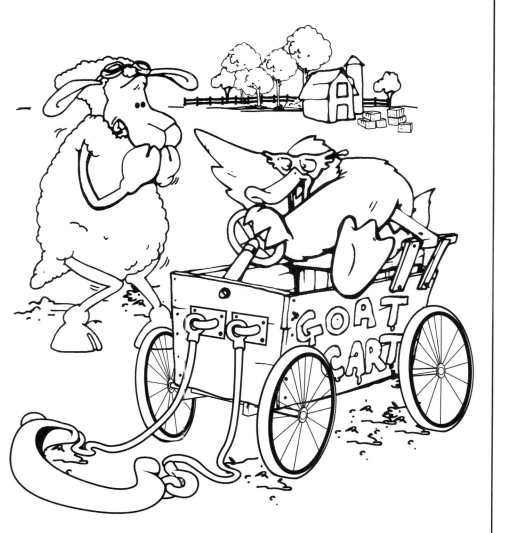

McGraw Hill SRA

"where are you gōing?" asked mack.

"come with mē. you will sēē," said sam.

"whȳ is there pāint on your hat and top and pants?" asked mack.

"come with mē. you will sēē," said sam.

"what is in the box?" asked mack.

"come with mē. you will sēē," said sam.

sō mack went with sam.

when they got to the park, sam went to a spot in the sun. it was nēar a trēē and a pond.

"stand hēre, mack," said sam.

"whȳ?" asked mack.

"you will sēē," answered sam.

sam got a brush. hē got pāint. hē got a pad.

"now stand still," said sam.

"whȳ?" asked mack. "it is tīme to tell mē."

"I am gōing to pāint you," answered sam.

"nō," said mack. "nō. nō. I let you do some funny things, sam. but you are not gōing to pāint mē. I don't want pāint on mē because I will have to tāke a bath."

"I am not gōing to get pāint on you. I am gōing to pāint on this pad. I will pāint what you look līke. I will not get pāint on you, but I will get some mōre pāint on mē," said sam.

"you had better not get pāint on mē," said mack.

"then hōld still and let mē pāint," said sam.

sam and mack are not brothers. sam is a duck. mack is a dog. but they are līke brothers. they līke ēach other. they are with ēach other every dāy.

the other dāy, mack and sam were walking. sam had a big box. sam had on a funny hat and top and pants. there was a lot of pāint on the hat and the top and the pants.

www.sraonline.com

Printed in the United States of America.

Send all inquiries to:
SRA/McGraw-Hill
4400 Easton Commons
Columbus, OH 43219

sam pāinted. pāint was flȳing every where. pāint got on sam. pāint got on the trēē. pāint got on the pad. pāint got on mack, but don't tell him.

"there. do you want to sēē what you look līke?" asked sam.

"what? that is not mē. I don't look līke that. I don't have a red tāil. I don't have a whīte nōse. I don't have pāint on mȳ ēars," mack yelled.

"you do now," said sam.

mack is painted

by Jane Gold
Illustrated by Brad Mancuso

Decodable Book Lesson 29

McGraw Hill SRA

mother tiger was under a trēē. it looked like shē was slēēping. but shē was not really slēēping.

"sh-sh-sh," said rocks. "mother is slēēping. let's jump on her."

rocks and socks ran and jumped on mom. mom and rocks and socks plāyed and plāyed. mom licked them and gāve them hugs.

after a little bit, they stopped and went to slēēp in the sun.

when they got up from slēēping, rocks said to her mom, "let's gō swimming. wē can gō hōme with socks. wē can swim in her pool."

so mom and rocks and socks started walking. when they got to a strēam, rocks said, "mom, let us rīde on your back, and you can swim."

"you girls can swim. but you think it is fun to rīde on mȳ back. you are funny. hōld on. here wē gō," said mom.

soon socks yelled, "there is mȳ hōme. there is mȳ pool."

they ran to the pool. rocks and socks jumped in. mom sat bȳ the pool.

rocks and socks plāyed in the pool. they went up and down the slīde.

"it is a hot, hot dāy. come to mȳ hōme and plāy in the water. wē can jump and slīde in the pool," said socks.

"let's ask mom," said rocks. "shē will gō with us."

www.sraonline.com

McGraw-Hill SRA

Printed in the United States of America.

Send all inquiries to:
SRA/McGraw-Hill
4400 Easton Commons
Columbus, OH 43219

when the sun started to gō down, mom said, "wē must gō now, rocks. it is tīme to gō hōme."

rocks started to crȳ. "don't crȳ, rocks. big girls don't crȳ ōver things līke that. wē will plāy another tīme."

then rocks ran hōme with her mother. and socks went into her hōme.

socks and rocks gō swimming

by Rain Park
Illustrated by Brad Mancuso

Decodable Book Lesson 24

McGraw Hill SRA

little tiger walked ōver to the little dog. shē looked at the dog from nōse to tāil. "can I pet him?" little tiger said to her mother.

"can little tiger pet you?" mother said to the little dog.

"arf. arf," little dog barked.

"hē said yes, little tiger."

little tiger smiled at the little dog. then little dog jumped up and kissed little tiger on the nōse.

"hē kissed mē. hē kissed mē. I līke him. what is his nāme? look at his fēēt. his fēēt look līke hē has socks. is his nāme socks?"

"arf. arf. arf," said the little dog.

mother tiger smiled. "hē is not a hē, little tiger. hē is a dog. her nāme is jāne. but shē says the nāme socks is better."

"arf."

"arf? what do you mēan? arf? whȳ do you talk līke that?" said little tiger.

"hē is a dog. hē is barking," said mother tiger.

"is that what a dog looks līke? hē looks līke a mop to mē," said little tiger.

"a dog can look līke that," said her mother.

www.sraonline.com

Printed in the United States of America.

Send all inquiries to:
SRA/McGraw-Hill
4400 Easton Commons
Columbus, OH 43219

“arf. arf. arf,” said jāne.

mother said to tiger, “jāne says you rock. so rocks is the nāme fōr you. now you are socks and rocks.”

then mother said, “socks you can tēach rocks to talk dog talk. rocks, you can tēach socks to talk tiger talk. you will have fun.”

socks and rocks

by Rain Park
Illustrated by Brad Manscuso

Decodable Book Lesson 19

McGraw Hill SRA

yarn went every where. hēre. there. every where. red yarn. whīte yarn. thōse chicks. they were having fun.

sam and dan and I hid under a pīle of hats.

miss tan and slīder yelled,
"stop, chicks. get back into the
box now."

"I must get mȳ yarn. then wē
must gō hōme," said miss tan.
"boys, I nēēd help. will you tāke
the chicks sō I can shop?"

miss tan and slīder did not
sēē the chicks flȳ up into the
yarn. they did not sēē the chicks
digging in a big pīle of yarn. they
did not sēē the chicks dīve into a
box of red yarn.

www.sraonline.com

Mc Graw Hill SRA

Printed in the United States of America.

Send all inquiries to:
SRA/McGraw-Hill
4400 Easton Commons
Columbus, OH 43219

sam and dan and I took the chicks fōr a little walk. the chicks went to slēēp in the box. then wē went back to the shop.

dan took the yarn fōr miss tan. miss tan took the box of chicks. then dan walked hōme with miss tan and the chicks.

after miss tan went, slīder sat down on the rug. "mȳ, mȳ, mȳ," shē said. "look at this shop."

"wē will fix it," said sam. "it will bē fīne."

and wē did fix it, and the shop was fīne.

the yarn shop part 2

by Mack Shore
Illustrated by Timothy Pack

Decodable Book Lesson 14

McGraw Hill SRA

sam has lots of nāmes: sam ron will mack moon chip. when his mother gets mad, shē says, "sam ron will mack moon chip, where are you?" then sam runs as fast as hē can to the pond.

his mother is slīder moon chip. shē has a yarn shop. shē has lots and lots of yarn. shē can not walk fast in her shop. shē can not run in her shop. shē has red socks sō shē can slīde. slīding is faster than walking.

sam and dan and I went to the yarn shop. wē were wet from the rāin. there was a lot of mud on us. slīder yelled, "wīpe your fēēt. dōn't get mud on the yarn. come give mē a hug. you nēēd to bē fatter. hēre, ēat a cōrn tart." wē līke slīder. shē is fun.

sam is a duck. hē runs the farm. Well, wē let him think hē runs the farm. wē līke sam.

www.sraonline.com

McGraw-Hill SRA

Printed in the United States of America.

Send all inquiries to:
SRA/McGraw-Hill
4400 Easton Commons
Columbus, OH 43219

miss tan and her chicks cāme into the shop. the chicks were slēēping in a box. miss tan got lots of yarn fōr hats and socks. miss tan and slīder were talking when the chicks jumped from the box.

the yarn shop part I

by Mack Shore

Illustrated by Timothy Pack

Decodable Book Lesson 9

McGraw Hill SRA

the duck jumped on the gōat that jumped on the cow that jumped on the bed.

"dōn't jump on the bed," mother said.

the kitten jumped on the duck that jumped on the gōat that jumped on the cow that jumped on the bed.

"dōn't jump on the bed," mother said.

the bug jumped on the kitten that jumped on the duck that jumped on the gōat that jumped on the cow that jumped on the bed.

"dōn't jump on the bed," mother said.

1

“ōh, nō, bug. you brōke the bed,” they said.

the bug fell on the rug.

the kitten fell on the bug that fell on the rug.

the duck fell on the kitten that fell on the bug that fell on the rug.

the gōat fell on the duck that fell on the kitten that fell on the bug that fell on the rug.

the cow fell on the gōat that fell on the duck that fell on the kitten that fell on the bug that fell on the rug.

the cow jumped on the bed.

“dōn’t jump on the bed,” mother said.

the gōat jumped on the cow that jumped on the bed.

“dōn’t jump on the bed,” mother said.

www.sraonline.com

McGraw-Hill SRA

Printed in the United States of America.

Send all inquiries to:
SRA/McGraw-Hill
4400 Easton Commons
Columbus, OH 43219

"the little bug," said mother. "What did you do to the little bug?"

"Where is the bug?" said the kitten.

"Where is the bug?" said the duck.

"Where is the bug?" said the gōat.

"ōh," said the cow. "hēre hē is. that bug bit mȳ ēar."

"sēē, I tōld you not to jump on the bed," said mother.

don't jump on the bed

by Moon Rocks
Illustrated by Brad Mancuso

Decodable Book Lesson 4

SRA

Para Usted y su Hijo(a) . . . . .

Se puede compartir el placer de leer independiente con su hijo(a). De cuando en cuando su hijo(a) traerá a casa su propio *Decodable Books* para leer con usted. Con su ayuda, estos cuentos le pueden dar a su hijo(a) práctica en la lectura importante y una alegre experiencia.

El Sistema Reading Mastery

En estos cuentos se usa un alfabeto especial para representar los sonidos de inglés De esta manera los estudiantes empiezan a leer en el programa ***Reading Mastery*** y es bastante fácil. El alfabeto especial les da a los estudiantes las pistas a los sonidos. Por ejemplo, cuando una letra representa el sonido de un vocal larga hay una línea recta sobre la letra y un "e mudo" ane se representa con un "e" pequeño. Los recuerdos ayudan a los estudiantes a evitar algunos de los problemas típicos de lectores inexpertos, como invertir las letras "d" y "b" y también reconocer cuál es el sonido de la letra "a" en ciertas palabras como "at" y "ate".

También la única letra mayúscula que se enseña en Grado K es el pronombre *"I"*. Muchas letras mayúsculas son muy distintas a las mismas letras minúsculas, incluyendo Aa, Bb, Dd, Ee, Ff, Gg, Hh, Ii, Ll, Nn, Qq, y Rr. Cada letra mayúscula exige instrucción especial. Al dejar que los estudiantes enfoquen en un sonido para cada símbolo, los estudiantes pronto empezarán a leer cuentos interesantes rápidamente.

Leyendo con su Hijo(a)

Si usted quiere reservar algunos minutos por la tarde para leer juntos los cuentos, aquí hay algunas sugerencias interesantes:

- No espere que su hijo(a) sepa leer perfectamente cada cuento. Concéntrese en leer el libro juntos.
- Participe usted leyendo parte del cuento.
- Si su hijo(a) no conoce alguna palabra, dígale la palabra y pídale que la pronuncie. Entonces vuelva a leer la frase otra vez.
- Discuta los cuentos, dé mucho ánimo y verá como su hijo(a) llegará a ser más fluente.

Aprender a leer exige mucha práctica. Compartir los cuentos es una manera de ganar experiencia. Esta colección será una biblioteca de libros que su hijo(a) podrá leer muchas veces. Escuche a su hijo(a) leer. Unos pocos minutos leyendo juntos cada día pueden proveer el interés, el entusiasmo, y la confianza que le hace falta para sobresalir en la lectura.

Un mensaje de ______________________________

For you and your child . . .

You can share the joy of independent reading with your child. From time to time your child will bring home his or her own *Decodable Takehome Books* to read with you. With your help, these stories can give your child important reading practice and a joyful shared reading experience.

The Reading Mastery System

In these stories there is an unusual way to represent the sounds of English. This is the way students begin reading in the ***Reading Mastery*** program, and it is surprisingly easy. The unusual elements give students clues to the sounds. For example, when a letter stands for a long vowel sound there is a straight line above it, and a "silent *e*" is represented by a small *e* (**cāke**).

Also, the only capital letter taught in Grade K is the pronoun *I*. This allows students to focus on learning the relationships of sounds and symbols and on comprehension without other concerns.

This system is used throughout Grade K and into Grade 1. It "fades" to our conventional system beginning in Lesson 81 of Grade 1.

Reading with Your Child

You might want to set aside a few minutes each evening to read these stories together. Here are some suggestions you might find helpful:

- Do not expect your child to read each story perfectly. Concentrate on sharing the book together.
- Participate by doing some of the reading.
- If your child gets stuck on a word, just say the word and ask the child to reread the sentence.
- Talk about the stories as you read, give lots of encouragement, and watch your child become more fluent.

Learning to read takes lots of practice. Sharing these stories is one way that your child can gain that valuable experience. Encourage your child to keep the books in a special place. This collection will become a library of books that your child can read and reread. Take the time to listen to your child read. Just a few moments of shared reading each day can give your child the interest, enthusiasm, and confidence needed to excel in reading.

A message from ______________________________________

5. Check to make sure the pages are in order.

100
mom is mad at him now. nō dog digs a lot. hē digs in thē mud.
4
sēē thōse tracks on thē rug? nō dog māde thōse tracks. mom got mad. mom said, "nō, dog, nō." nō dog had to gō to his hut.
5

6. Staple the pages along the fold.

nō dog digs
NO DOG
by Art Little
Illustrated by Timothy Pack
Decodable Book Lesson 127
Mc Graw Hill SRA

How to Make a Takehome Book

1. Tear out the pages you need.
2. Place pages 4 and 5 and pages 2 and 7 face up.

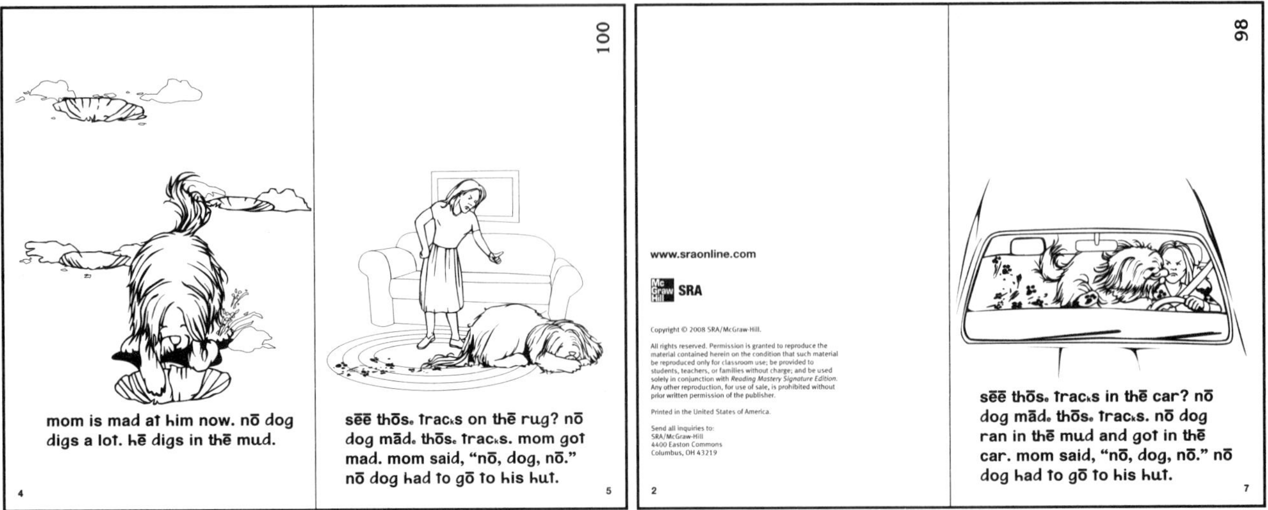

3. Place pages 4 and 5 on top of pages 2 and 7.

4. Fold along the center line.

About the Decodable Takehome Books

The *Decodable Takehome Books* provide opportunities for your students to apply the skills and vocabulary they learn in the ***Reading Mastery*** program as they read independently. The stories also use the orthography used at this level of the ***Reading Mastery*** program. The vocabulary in these stories is ten lessons behind the vocabulary in the corresponding ***Reading Mastery*** lessons so students will have had many opportunities to practice reading the words before reading the *Decodable Takehome Books*.

Students can fold and staple the pages of each *Decodable Takehome Book* to make books of their own to keep and read. We suggest you keep extra sets of the stories in your classroom for the students to reread.

Directions for preparing the books are on pages 6 and 7.

Contents

SRAonline.com

SRA

Printed in the United States of America.

Send all inquiries to this address:
SRA/McGraw-Hill
4400 Easton Commons
Columbus, OH 43219

ISBN: 978-0-07-612482-4
MHID: 0-07-612482-7

5 6 7 8 9 RHR 13 12 11

The McGraw·Hill Companies

SRA

Practice De
Stories Blackline Master Book

Grade 1

Columbus, OH

They walked a long time. At last, the two men got to a clearing. The moon shone down on little men playing long pins. The men had long hair and long beards. They wore big hats, long coats, and short pants.

The game stopped. The men looked at Rip. Then they went back to their long pins. There was no sound but the rolling balls crashing into the pins, like thunder in the mountains.

A long time ago, Rip Van Winkle lived in a little town. Everyone loved Rip. He was a kind man who loved to laugh and play with the children. He always had time to help others or tell stories.

One day, Rip and Wolf, his dog, were walking along the river in the mountains. Late in the afternoon, they stopped under a tree to watch the river.

Clouds piled up over the mountains and the sky turned gray. Rip turned to head home. Then someone called, "Rip Van Winkle. Rip Van Winkle." Rip stopped. He looked around. Maybe it was the wind.

A little man carrying a big sack walked slowly to Rip. He asked Rip to help him carry the sack. As they went along, Rip could hear a strange sound, like thunder in the mountains. He grew more afraid.

Judith took Rip home. Soon Rip was back to his old ways. And to this day when the thunder rolls, people say, "Rip's little friends are bowling again."

Rip Van Winkle Part 2

by Washington Irving
retold

Decodable Book Lesson 119

McGraw Hill SRA

www.sraonline.com

Printed in the United States of America.

Send all inquiries to:
SRA/McGraw-Hill
4400 Easton Commons
Columbus, OH 43219

"Rip Van Winkle. But he left over 20 years ago."

"And who is that under the tree?"

"That is my brother, Rip Van Winkle."

Then Rip told his story, and most people didn't believe it. But it didn't matter because it was a good story.

"I don't know who I am," answered Rip. "I believe I am Rip Van Winkle, but you tell me that Rip Van Winkle is sleeping under that tree."

Just then a woman and her baby passed. "Hush, Rip," she said to her baby.

Rip turned to her. He said, "What is your name?"

"Judith," she answered.

"And your father? What is his name?" asked Rip.

Rip tried to get up, but he was sore so he got up very slowly. He called for Wolf, but Wolf didn't come. And what had happened to the path that led to the town? It was overgrown with grass and trees. Slowly, Rip worked his way to the town. He couldn't understand why he felt so old.

As Rip got near town, he met many people, but they just looked at him. He didn't know them, and they didn't know him. Rip stopped and looked and rubbed his chin. His chin? On his chin was a long, white beard. Rip was scared. What was the matter? How could this be the town he just left?

In fear, Rip walked to his farm. He hoped to hear his children playing in the yard. He hoped to hear his wife yelling at him to get to work. There was nothing but an old house.

Rip ran back to town. People stood around him. At last, Rip asked, "Does anyone here know Rip Van Winkle?"

"Yes, we do," someone said. "There he is sitting under that tree in the park."

The man under the tree looked just as Rip had when he went to the mountains. The man turned back to Rip and asked, "Who are you, old man? Where did you come from?"

When the gardener came back the next day, the little trees were all dead.

The Silly Monkeys

A Jataka story

Decodable Book Lesson 124

McGraw Hill SRA

www.sraonline.com

Printed in the United States of America.

Send all inquiries to:
SRA/McGraw-Hill
4400 Easton Commons
Columbus, OH 43219

Then those silly monkeys pulled up all the little trees to see which trees had long roots and which had short roots.

When the sun went down, the monkeys took the watering cans and began to water the little trees. "See that each little tree has enough water," said the boss monkey.

"How will we know when each little tree has enough?" they asked. The boss of the monkeys had no good answer, so he said, "Pull up each little tree and look at its roots. Give a lot of water to those with long roots, but only a little to those trees with short roots."

Once upon a time a king gave a holiday to all the people in one of his cities.

The king's gardener said to himself: "All my friends are having a holiday in the city. I could go into the city and have fun with them if I did not have to water the little trees in this garden. I know what I'll do. I'll get the monkeys to water the trees for me." In those days, monkeys lived in the king's garden.

So the gardener went to the boss monkey, and said: "You are lucky monkeys to be living in the king's garden. You have a fine place to play in. You have the best food. You have no work at all to do. You can play all day, every day. Today my friends are having a holiday in the city, and I want to have fun with them. Will you water the little trees so that I can go away?"

"Oh, yes!" said the boss monkey. "We will be glad to do that."

"Don't forget to water the trees when the sun goes down. See they have enough water, but not more than enough," said the gardener. Then he showed them where the watering cans were kept, and he went away.

The other animals could hear the lion, and they ran to him. But no one could think of what to do.

The little mouse ran to him. She ran up the tree and out onto the net. She chewed on the ropes. In no time, she chewed the ropes, and the lion was free.

The lion was very happy. He told the mouse, "You're a very brave mouse. Thank you for helping me. I will never laugh at you again."

Two Tales

The Ant and the Grasshopper

&

The Lion and the Mouse

by Aesop

Decodable Book Lesson 129

www.sraonline.com

SRA

Printed in the United States of America.

Send all inquiries to:
SRA/McGraw-Hill
4400 Easton Commons
Columbus, OH 43219

"Wait!" she shouted. "Don't eat me, please. If you will let me go, I will help you."

The lion laughed. How could a mouse help a lion? Well, he was not hungry, so he let her go and went back to sleep.

The little mouse ran away as fast as her legs would carry her.

Many days later the lion fell into a net and was trapped. No matter how hard he tried, he couldn't get out. The lion began to roar. He roared and he roared and he roared.

The Lion and the Mouse

A long time ago, there was a mean lion. One day, he ate a big lunch. Then he went to his den to take a nap.

As the lion was sleeping, a little mouse was looking for seeds. She ran smack into the lion's nose and woke him. The mouse tried to run away, but the lion got her by the tail.

The Ant and the Grasshopper

Once upon a time, a grasshopper was hopping around, chirping and singing, singing and chirping. An ant passed by, carrying a big seed of corn.

"Ant," said the grasshopper, "rest a minute. Let's talk a while."

"No time for chit-chat," said the ant as she rushed on. "No time at all. I must get food put away for the winter. You should do the same."

"Oh, winter is a long way off, and there is lots of food," said the grasshopper.

The next day as the grasshopper was hopping around, chirping and singing, singing and chirping, the ant passed by again. This time she was carrying a grain of wheat.

"Ant," said the grasshopper, "rest a minute. Let's talk a while."

"No time for chit-chat," said the ant as she rushed on. "No time at all. I must get food put away for the winter. You should do the same."

"Oh, winter is a long way off, and there is lots of food," said the grasshopper.

And so it went, day after day. The ant worked. The grasshopper played.

Winter came, as it always does. The plants died, and the grasshopper could not find any food.

The ant was snug in her home with a lot to eat. And the grasshopper? Well, the grasshopper got colder and colder because it was not ready for winter.

The Wind in the Willows

Chapter 1
THE RIVER BANK
Part 1

by Kenneth Grahame
retold
illustrated by Artifact Group

Decodable Book Lesson 134

McGraw Hill SRA

www.sraonline.com

SRA

Printed in the United States of America.

Send all inquiries to:
SRA/McGraw-Hill
4400 Easton Commons
Columbus, OH 43219

Rat said nothing. He bent down and grabbed a rope and pulled on it. Then he stepped into a little boat which Mole had not seen. It was painted blue outside and white inside. And it was just the size for two animals. Mole's heart went out to it at once, even if he didn't know what it was for.

Rat rowed across and made fast. Then he held up a paw as the Mole stepped down. "Lean on me!" he said. "Now then, step carefully!" Mole found himself seated in the rear of a real boat.

A brown little face, with whiskers. A round face, with a twinkle in its eye. Small neat ears and thick soft hair.

It was Water Rat!

Then the two animals stood and looked at each other.

“Hello, Mole!” said Water Rat.

“Hello, Rat!” said Mole.

“Would you like to come over?” asked Rat.

“Oh, well, that’s easy for you to say,” said Mole.

Mole had been working very hard all morning. He was cleaning his little home. Spring was moving in the air and in the ground and all around him. Suddenly he flung his brush to the floor. He said “O blow!” and also “Hang spring cleaning!” Then he ran out of the house without putting on his coat. Something was calling him. So he dug and dug till at last, pop! His snout came out into the sunshine. He found himself rolling in the warm grass.

“This is fine!” he said to himself. The sunshine struck hot on his fur. A soft wind touched his face. After a long, long winter in the ground, he ran across the grass to the road.

"Hold up!" said an old rabbit. "One dime to pass on this road!" "Onion-sauce! Onion-sauce! Onion-sauce!" Mole said. He was off before the rabbits could think what to say. Then they said to each other: "How silly you are! Why didn't you tell him—" and so on. But, of course, it was much too late.

Suddenly Mole stood beside a river. Never in his life had he seen a river. By the side of the river he ran. And when he was tired at last, he sat on the bank, while the river still chattered to him.

He saw a dark hole in the bank on the other side of the river. "What a nice home that hole would be," he said to himself. Something small seemed to twinkle down in the hole. It went away. Then it twinkled once more like a little star. Then, as he looked, it winked at him. An eye. A small face grew up around it, like a frame around a window.

The Wind in the Willows

Chapter 1
THE RIVER BANK
Part 2

by Kenneth Grahame
retold
illustrated by Artifact Group

Decodable Book Lesson 139

McGraw Hill SRA

www.sraonline.com

SRA

Printed in the United States of America.

Send all inquiries to:
SRA/McGraw-Hill
4400 Easton Commons
Columbus, OH 43219

Mole never heard a word he was saying. He trailed a paw in the water and dreamed long waking dreams. Water Rat, like the good little fellow he was, rowed on and let Mole dream.

“Put that under your feet,” he said to Mole. Then he untied the rope and rowed off again.

“What’s inside it?” asked Mole.

“There is cold chicken inside it,” answered Rat. “Cold ham, cold beef, pickles, rolls, water—”

“O stop, stop,” cried Mole. “This is too much!”

“Do you really think so?” asked Rat. “It’s only what I always take on these little trips.”

“This is a wonderful day!” said Mole, as Rat started rowing again. “Do you know, I’ve never been in a boat before in all my life.”

“What?” cried Rat. “Never been in a—you never—well, what have you been doing, then?”

“Is it so nice as all that?” asked Mole.

“Nice? It’s the only thing,” said Water Rat. “Believe me, my friend, there is nothing as much fun as messing about in boats.”

“Look ahead, Rat!” cried Mole.

It was too late. The boat struck the bank. Rat lay on his back at the bottom of the boat, his heels in the air.

Rat went on, picking himself up with a laugh. “In or out of them, it doesn’t matter. Nothing seems really to matter. Whether you get away or whether you don’t; whether you reach your goal or whether you reach somewhere else, or whether you never get anywhere at all, you’re always doing something. But you never really do anything. And when you’ve done it, there’s always something else to do. And you can do it if you like, but you are better off not doing it. Look here! If you’ve really nothing else to do this morning we can go down the river and have a long day of it?”

 12

Mole leaned back into the soft pillows. “What a day I’m having!” he said. “Let us start at once!”

“Hold on a minute, then!” said Rat. He tied the rope through a ring in his dock. Then he disappeared into his home. After a time, he came out carrying a big basket.

The Wind in the Willows

Chapter 1
THE OPEN ROAD
Part 3

by Kenneth Grahame
retold
illustrated by Artifact Group

Decodable Book Lesson 142

McGraw Hill SRA

www.sraonline.com

Printed in the United States of America.

Send all inquiries to:
SRA/McGraw-Hill
4400 Easton Commons
Columbus, OH 43219

"And on past the Wild Wood?" he asked.

"On past the Wild Wood comes the Wide World," said Rat. "And that's something that doesn't matter, either to you or me. I've never been there, and I'm never going. You won't either if you've got any brains at all. Don't ever speak of it again, please. Now then! Here is our backwater at last, where we are going to lunch."

"Why, who should mess with him?" asked Mole.

"Well, of course—there—are others," answered Rat. "Foxes and so on. They are all right in a way. I'm very good friends with them. Pass the time of day when we meet. But they act out sometimes, and then you can't really trust them, and that's the fact."

"I like your coat, old chap," Rat said after some time had passed. "I'm going to get a black coat myself some day."

"I'm sorry," said Mole. "But all this is so new to me. So—this—is—a—River!"

"The River," said Rat.

"And you really live by the river? What a happy life!"

"By it and with it and on it and in it," said Rat. "It's brother and sister to me. And food and drink and washing. It's my world, and I don't want any other. Oh! The times we have had! Any time of the year, the river is fun."

“But is it a bit boring at times?” Mole asked. “Just you and the river, and no one else to pass a word with?”

“No one else to—well, I must not be hard on you,” said Rat. “You’re new to it, and you don’t know. The bank is so crowded now days that many people are moving away. Oh no, it is not what it used to be, at all. Always someone wanting you to do something. As if a fellow had nothing else to do!”

“What lies over there?” asked Mole, waving a paw at a woodland on one side of the river.

“That? Oh, that’s just the Wild Wood,” said Rat. “We don’t go there very much, we river-bankers.”

“Are the people in there not very nice?” said Mole.

“W…e…ll,” answered Rat, “let me see. Most of them are all right. And the rabbits—some of them. But rabbits are a mixed lot. And then there is Badger, of course. He lives right in the middle of it; wouldn’t live anywhere else, either, if you paid him to do it. Dear old Badger! Nobody messes with him. They had better not,” he added.

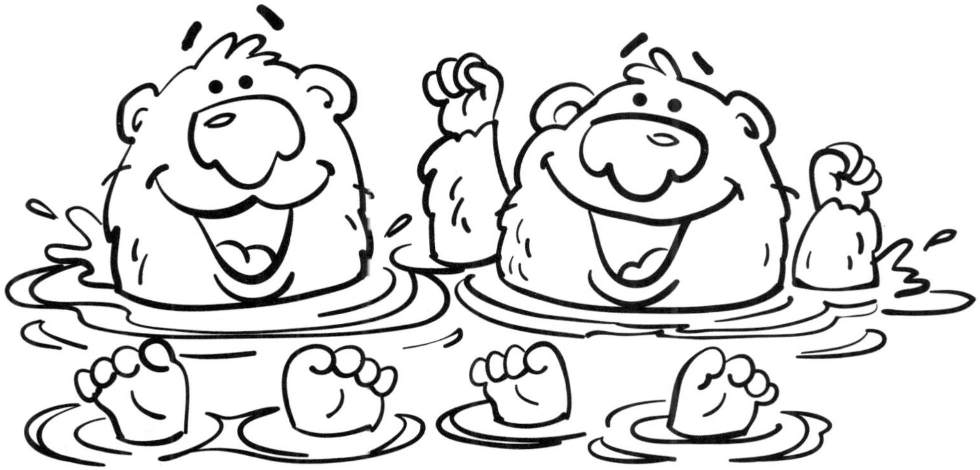

The Wind in the Willows

Chapter 1
THE OPEN ROAD
Part 4

by Kenneth Grahame
retold
illustrated by Artifact Group

Decodable Book Lesson 144

SRA

www.sraonline.com

McGraw-Hill SRA

Printed in the United States of America.

Send all inquiries to:
SRA/McGraw-Hill
4400 Easton Commons
Columbus, OH 43219

“That’s just the sort of fellow he is!” said Rat. “Hates to be around others! Now we won’t see any more of him today. Well, tell us, who is out on the river?”

“Toad’s out, for one,” answered Otter. “In his brand new racing boat!”

The two animals looked at each other and laughed.

“Once, it was nothing but sailing,” said Rat. “And a nice mess he made of it. Last year it was house-boating. We all had to go and stay with him in his house-boat. He was going to spend the rest of his life in a house-boat. It’s all the same, whatever he takes up; he gets tired of it, and starts on something new.”

"Proud to meet you," said Otter, and the two animals were friends.

"So much going on!" said Otter. "All the world seems to be out on the river today. I came up this backwater to try and get a little peace. Then I met you fellows."

There was a sound behind them. Coming from a bush a striped head and a big neck, stared at them.

"Come on, old Badger!" shouted Rat.

The Badger trotted turned his back and disappeared.

Leaving the main stream, they now passed into what seemed like a little lake. Green grass sloped down on each side, brown tree roots showed under the still water. Ahead of them was a dripping mill wheel and mill house and little clear chattering voices. It was so very pretty that Mole could only hold up his front paws and say, "Oh my! Oh my! Oh my!"

Rat took the boat to the bank, tied it, helped Mole safely on shore, and swung out the lunch basket. Mole begged to take it out all by himself. Rat was very pleased to let him and to lie on the grass and rest.

When all was ready, Rat said, "Now, give me a hand, old fellow!" Mole was very glad to obey, for he had started his spring-cleaning very early that morning. And he had not had a bite to eat from that time that seemed to be so many days ago.

"What are you looking at?" said Rat after they had a bit to eat.

"I am looking," said Mole, "at a streak of bubbles that I see along the top of the water. That is a thing that strikes me as funny."

"Bubbles? Oh, oh!" said Rat, and chirped.

A wide shining nose showed over the bank. Then Otter pulled himself out and shook the water from his coat.

"Did you eat all the food?" he said, going for the food. "Why didn't you ask me to come, Ratty?"

"We didn't know we were going to do it," answered Rat. "By the way, this is my friend Mr. Mole."

The Wind in the Willows

Chapter 1
THE OPEN ROAD
Part 5

by Kenneth Grahame
retold
illustrated by Artifact Group

Decodable Book Lesson 147

www.sraonline.com

Printed in the United States of America.

Send all inquiries to:
SRA/McGraw-Hill
4400 Easton Commons
Columbus, OH 43219

Mole was still for a minute or two. But he began to feel more and more jealous of Rat. His pride began to think that he could do it every bit as well. He jumped up and grabbed the oars. Rat was taken by surprise and fell back off his seat with his legs in the air. And Mole took his place and grabbed the oars. He knew that he could row the boat.

"Stop it, you silly thing!" cried Rat, from the bottom of the boat. "You can't do it! You'll turn us over!"

The afternoon sun was getting low as Rat rowed home. He was day dreaming and not watching Mole. But Mole was very full of lunch, and pride. And he was already at home in a boat. Soon he said, "Ratty! Please, I want to row, now!"

Rat shook his head with a smile. "Not yet, my friend," he said. "Wait till you've had a few lessons. It's not so easy as it looks."

From where they sat, Mole and Rat could just see the main stream across the land. Just then a racing boat appeared. The rower was splashing badly and rolling a good deal, but working his hardest. Rat stood up and called him, but Toad shook his head and got to his work.

"He'll be out of the boat in a minute if he rolls like that," said Rat, sitting down again.

"Of course he will," laughed Otter.

A Mayfly flashed over the river. A swirl of water and a "cloop!" and the Mayfly was gone.

So was Otter.

Mole looked down. The voice was still in his ears, but Otter was not to be seen.

But again there was a streak of bubbles on the river.

"Well, well," said Rat, "I think we should be moving. I wonder which of us had better pack the lunch basket."

"O, please let me," said Mole. So, of course, Rat let him.

Putting things back into the basket was not such fun as taking them out. It never is. But Mole liked everything. Just when he had got the basket packed and strapped up, he saw a plate staring up at him from the grass. And when the job had been done again, Rat showed the Mole a spoon that anybody should have seen. And last of all, the jam pot, which he had been sitting on without knowing it. Still, somehow, the thing got finished at last, without anyone getting mad.

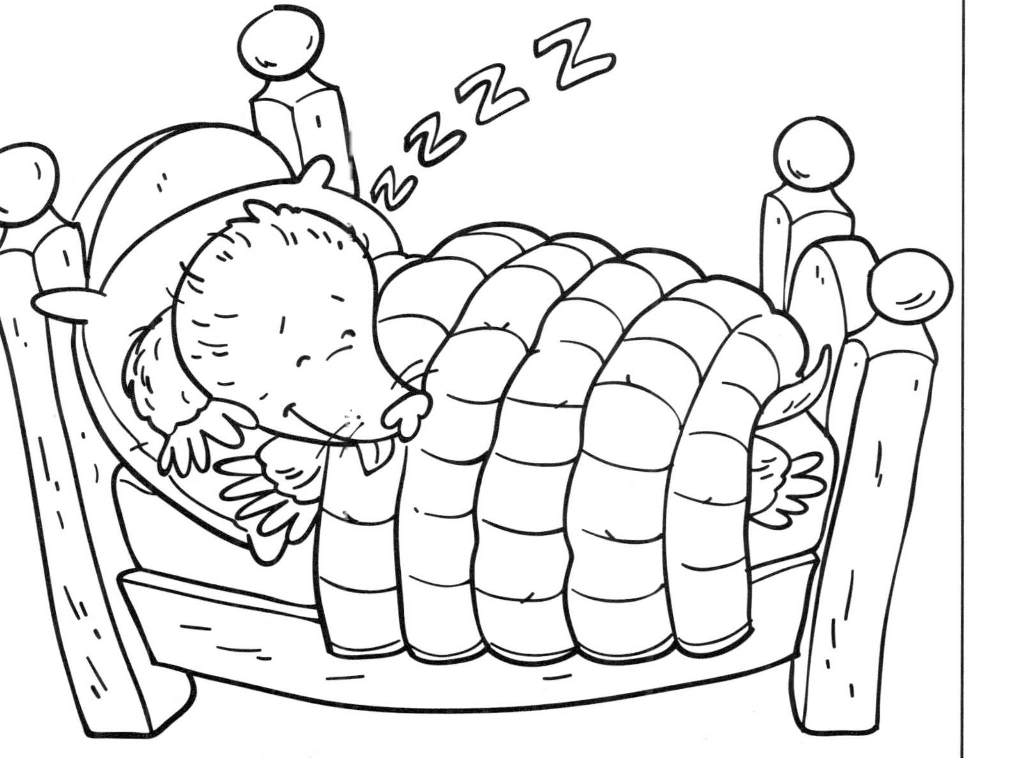

This day was only the first of many for Mole. Each of them longer and full of fun as summer moved on.

The Wind in the Willows

Chapter 1
THE OPEN ROAD
Part 6

by Kenneth Grahame
retold
Illustrated by Artifact Group

Decodable Book Lesson 149

SRA

www.sraonline.com

SRA

Printed in the United States of America.

Send all inquiries to:
SRA/McGraw-Hill
4400 Easton Commons
Columbus, OH 43219

Mole was so touched by his kind manner of speaking that he could not answer him. He had to brush away a tear or two with the back of his paw. But Rat looked the other way. Soon Mole felt better again. He was even able to give some backtalk to some hens who were laughing to each other about the way he looked.

When they got home, Rat made a fire in the den, and planted the Mole in an armchair in front of it. He gave him a robe and slippers and told him river stories until dinner time. They were very thrilling stories, too. Stories about leaping fish and about flights down drains and night fishing with Otter or trips with Badger. Dinner was a most cheerful meal; but very shortly after that a sleepy Mole had to be taken upstairs to the best bedroom. He soon laid his head on his pillow in peace, knowing that his new friend the river was lapping at his window.

When all was ready for a start once more, Mole, sagging and wet, took his seat in the rear of the boat. As they set off, he said in a low voice, "Ratty, my good friend! I am very sorry for the way I acted. My heart stops when I think how we might not have found that lunch basket. I have been a silly thing, and I know it. Will you overlook it this once and forgive me, and let things go on as before?"

"That's all right!" answered Rat. "What's a little wet to a Water Rat? I'm more in the water than out of it most days. Don't you think anymore about it. I really think you had better come and stay with me for a little time. It's very plain, you know—not like Toad's house at all—but you haven't seen that yet. Still, I can make you feel at home. And I'll teach you to row and to swim, and you'll soon be as good on the water as any of us."

Mole flung his oars back with a grand show and made a dig at the water. He missed the water. His legs flew up over his head, and he found himself lying on top of the Rat. Very upset, he made a grab at the side of the boat, and then—Sploosh!

Over went the boat, and he found himself fighting in the river.

Oh my, how cold the water was, and oh, how very wet it felt. How it sang in his ears as he went down, down, down! How bright the sun looked as he rose to the top, gagging! How he lost hope when he felt himself sinking again! Then a strong paw gripped him by the back of his neck. It was Rat, and Rat was laughing. Mole could feel him laughing, right down his arm and through his paw, and so into his—Mole's—neck.

Rat got hold of an oar and put it under Mole's arm. Then he did the same to the other side of him. Then swimming behind Mole, Rat got Mole to shore. He pulled him out and set him down on the bank, a lump of gloom.

Rat rubbed him down a bit and got some of the wet out of him. Then he said, "Now old fellow! Trot up and down the path as hard as you can, till you're warm and dry again. I'll dive for the lunch basket."

So Mole trotted about until he was fairly dry, while Rat dived into the water again. He got the boat, turned it right side up, and tied it up. Then he little by little he got his floating things to shore. At last, he got the lunch basket and got to land with it.

Rounding a bend in the river, they came in sight of a handsome, old house of old red brick, with well-kept yards reaching down to the water.

"There is Toad Hall," said Rat; "and that creek on the left, where the sign says, "Keep out. No landing," leads to his boat house. We'll leave the boat there. The barns are over there to the right. That's the dinner hall. Very old, that is. Toad is rather rich, you know. This is really one of the nicest houses in these parts, but we never say so to Toad."

The Wind in the Willows

Chapter 2
THE OPEN ROAD
Part 1

by Kenneth Grahame
retold

Decodable Book Lesson 152

SRA

www.sraonline.com

McGraw-Hill SRA

Printed in the United States of America.

Send all inquiries to:
SRA/McGraw-Hill
4400 Easton Commons
Columbus, OH 43219

"Why, of course," said Rat, jumping to his feet. His song was gone from his mind for the day. "Get the boat out, and we'll row up there at once. It's always the right time to call on Toad. Early or late he is always the same fellow. Always glad to see you, always sorry when you go!"

"He must be a very nice animal," said Mole. He got into the boat and took the oars, while Rat seated himself in the rear.

"He is the best of animals," answered Rat. "So simple, so good, and so kind. Maybe he is not very smart—we can't all be smart. And maybe that he brags a lot. But he is a good friend."

"I don't know that I think so very much of that little song, Rat," said Mole.

"The ducks don't either," answered Rat cheerfully. "They think I should leave them alone to do what they want. They think I shouldn't make fun of them. That's what the ducks think."

"That's true. That's true," said Mole.

"No, it's not!" cried Rat.

"Well then, it's not, it's not," answered Mole. "But what I wanted to ask you was, won't you take me to call on Mr. Toad? Everyone has said so much about him, and I do so want to meet him."

"Ratty," said Mole suddenly, one bright summer morning. "If you please, I want to ask you to do something for me."

Rat was sitting on the river bank, singing a little song he had just made up. He was singing and not listening to Mole or anything else. From early morning he had been swimming in the river with the ducks. And when the ducks stood on their heads suddenly, as ducks will, he would dive down and tickle their necks, just under where their chins would be if ducks had chins. Then the ducks had to come up again fast. They were mad and shaking their feathers at him, for it is impossible to say all you feel when your head is under water. At last they begged him to go away and leave them alone. So Rat went away and sat on the river bank in the sun. He made up a song about them, which he called "DUCKS' DITTY."

All along the backwater,
Through the rushes tall,
Ducks are a-dabbling,
Up tails all!
Ducks' tails, drakes' tails,
Yellow feet a-quiver,
Yellow bills all out of sight
Feeding in the river!
Soft green weeds
Where the roach swim
Here we keep our store,
Cool and full and dim.

Everyone for what he likes!
We like to be
Heads down, tails up,
Dabbling free!
Up in the blue sky
Birds swirl and call—
We are down a-dabbling
Up tails all!

The Wind in the Willows

Chapter 2
THE OPEN ROAD
Part 2

by Kenneth Grahame
retold
Illustrated by Artifact Group

Decodable Book Lesson 154

McGraw Hill SRA

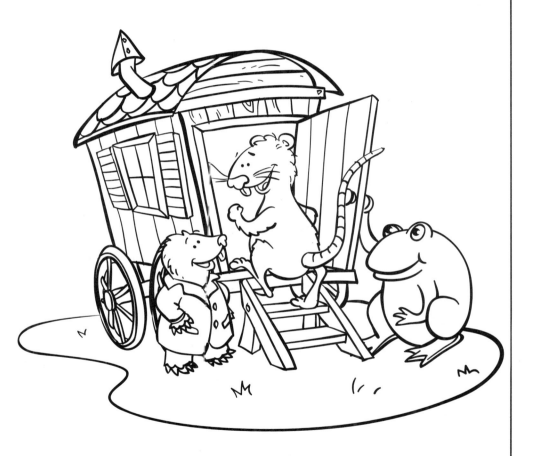

www.sraonline.com

McGraw-Hill SRA

Printed in the United States of America.

Send all inquiries to:
SRA/McGraw-Hill
4400 Easton Commons
Columbus, OH 43219

He led the way to the barn yard. And there, they saw a cart, painted yellow and green with red wheels.

"There you are!" cried Toad. "There is real life for you in that little cart. The open road, the dusty paths, camps, towns, cities! Here today, up and off to somewhere else the next day! The whole world before you. And mind you, this is the very finest cart of its sort that was ever built. Come inside and look at it. Planned it all myself, I did!"

"It's about your rowing, I think," said Rat. "You're getting on fairly well, though you splash a good bit still. With a lot of work, and a lot of teaching, you may . . ."

"O, pooh! Boating!" said Toad. "I gave that up long ago. A bad way to use time, that's what it is. It makes me downright sorry to see you fellows, who should know better, spending all your time in that way. No, I've found the real thing. I plan to give the rest of life to it. Come with me, dear Ratty, and your friend also, just as far as the barn yard. You will see what you will see!"

They rowed up the creek, and Mole slipped his oars as they passed near the boat house. Here they saw many handsome boats, hung from the cross beams, but none in the water. It seemed the no one used the place anymore.

Rat looked around him. "I understand," said Rat. "Boating is played out. He is tired of it and done with it. I wonder what new fad he has taken up now? Come along and let's look him up. We will hear all about it soon."

They got out and walked across the yard looking for Toad. They found him resting in a wicker garden chair, with a strange look on his face, and a big map spread out on his lap.

"Hooray!" he cried, jumping up on seeing them. "This is wonderful!" He shook their paws. "How kind of you!" he went on, dancing round them. "I was just going to send a boat down the river for you, Ratty. I want you badly—you and your friend. Now what will you take? Come inside and have something! You don't know how lucky it is, your turning up just now!"

"Let's sit a bit, Toady!" said Rat, throwing himself into an easy chair. Mole took another by the side of him and said something about Toad's home.

"Finest house on the whole river," cried Toad. "Or anywhere else, for that matter," he could not help adding.

Here Rat bumped Mole. Toad saw him do it, and turned very red. He said nothing. Then Toad started laughing. "All right, Ratty," he said. "It's only my way, you know. And it's not such a very bad house, is it? You know you rather like it yourself. Now, look here. You are the very animals I wanted. You've got to help me!"

"No, no, we'll see it out," answered Rat. "Thanks, but I should stick by Toad till this trip is ended. It wouldn't be safe for him to be left to himself. It won't take very long. His fads never do. Good night!"

The end was nearer than even Rat thought.

The Wind in the Willows

Chapter 2
THE OPEN ROAD
Part 3

by Kenneth Grahame
retold

Decodable Book Lesson 157

www.sraonline.com

SRA

Printed in the United States of America.

Send all inquiries to:
SRA/McGraw-Hill
4400 Easton Commons
Columbus, OH 43219

Late in the evening, they stopped and turned the horse out to eat. They ate their simple dinner sitting on the grass beside the cart. Toad talked big about all he was going to do in the days to come. The stars grew bigger all around them. A yellow moon appeared suddenly to listen to their talk. At last they turned in to their little bunks in the cart. Toad, kicking out his legs, said, “Well, good night, you fellows! This is the real life! Talk about your old river!”

“I don’t talk about my river,” answered Rat. “You know I don’t, Toad. But I think about it,” he added. “I think about it all the time!”

Mole reached out for Rat’s paw and gave it a squeeze. “I’ll do whatever you like, Ratty,” he said. “Should we run away in the morning and go back to our dear old hole on the river?”

When they were ready, Toad led his friends to the barn yard to get the old horse. The horse did not want the dusty job of pulling the cart. So it took a lot of chasing to get him. Meantime Toad packed the boxes with things they needed, and hung feed bags, nets of onions, hay, and baskets from the bottom of the cart. At last the horse was ready, and they set off. They were all talking at once. Each animal either walking by the side of the cart or sitting on the seat. It was a golden afternoon. The smell of the dust they kicked up was rich. Birds called to them. Other animals waved or stopped to say nice things about their cart. Rabbits, sitting at their front doors, held up their paws, and said, "O my! O my! O my!"

Mole was thrilled, and followed Toad up the steps and inside the cart. Rat only sniffed and put his hands deep into his pockets, staying where he was.

It was very handsome. Little sleeping bunks—a little table that folded up by the wall. A cooking-stove, lockers, books, a birdcage with a bird in it, and pots, pans, and jugs of every size and kind.

"All done!" said Toad, pulling open a locker. "You see, everything you can want. Soda-water here—note paper, jam, cards," he said, as they went down the steps again. "You'll find that I didn't forget anything, when we start this afternoon."

"I'm sorry," said Rat slowly, "but did I overhear you say something about "we" and "start" and "this afternoon"?"

"Now, you dear good old Ratty," said Toad. "Don't begin talking in that way, because you know you've got to come. I can't do it without you. You really don't mean to stick to your old river all your life, and just live in a hole in a bank, and boat? I want to show you the world! I'm going to make an animal of you, my boy!"

"I don't care," said Rat. "I'm not coming, and that's flat. And I am going to stick to my old river, and live in a hole, and boat, as I've always done. And what's more, Mole will stick me and do as I do, won't you, Mole?"

"Of course I will," said Mole. "I'll always stick with you, Rat, and what you say is to be. All the same, it sounds as if it might have been fun, you know!" he added. Oh, Mole! This life was so new to him, and so thrilling. And he did fall in love at first sight with the yellow cart.

Rat saw what was going on in Mole's mind. He hated upsetting people. He really liked Mole and would do almost anything for him. Toad was watching them.

"Come along in, and have some lunch," he said. "We'll talk it over. You don't have to make up your mind right now. Of course, I don't really care. I only want to please you fellows."

While they ate lunch, Toad let himself go. He talked about living on the road in such glowing colors that Mole could hardly sit still. Soon it seemed that they would take the trip. Rat didn't want to upset his two friends. Toad and Mole were already planning out each day in the weeks to come.

"You see what it is?" Rat said to Mole. "I give up. When we get to the town, we'll get a train to take us back to the river tonight."

The following evening, Mole was sitting on the bank fishing, when Rat came along. "Did you hear the news?" he asked. "There is nothing else being talked about all along the river bank. Toad went up to town this morning. And he is buying a big motor-car."

The Wind in the Willows

Chapter 2
THE OPEN ROAD
Part 4

by Kenneth Grahame
retold

Decodable Book Lesson 159

SRA

www.sraonline.com

SRA

Printed in the United States of America.

Send all inquiries to:
SRA/McGraw-Hill
4400 Easton Commons
Columbus, OH 43219

"But what about Toad?" asked Mole. "We can't leave him here, sitting in the middle of the road by himself. It's not safe. What if another Thing comes along?"

"Oh, forget Toad," said Rat. "I've done with him!"

They had not gone very far when there was a tapping of feet behind them.

"Now, look here, Toad!" said Rat. "As soon as we get to the town, you'll have to go to the police. See if they know anything about that motor-car. And then you'll have to find someone to get the cart and fix it. It will take time, but it can be fixed. Mole and I will go find rooms where we can stay till the cart's ready."

"Police! Police!" said Toad. "Fix the cart! I'm done with carts forever. I never want to see the cart, or to hear of it, again. Oh, Ratty! You can't think how happy I am that you came on this trip! I wouldn't have gone without you, and then I might never have seen that that motor-car!"

Rat shook him. "Are you coming to help us, Toad?" he asked.

"Wonderful sight!" said Toad. "The real way to travel! The only way to travel! Oh poop-poop! Oh my! Oh my!"

"Oh stop being so silly, Toad!" cried Mole.

"And to think I never knew!" went on Toad. "All these years, I never knew! But now that I know. Oh what a road lies before me! What dust clouds will spring up behind me as I speed on my way!"

"What are we to do with him?" Mole asked Water Rat.

"Nothing at all," answered Rat. "Because there is really nothing to be done. You see, I know him from of old. He has a new fad, and it always takes him that way at first. He'll continue like that for days now. Never mind him. Let's see what we can do about the cart."

The cart would go no longer. Rat took the horse. "Come on!" he said to the Mole. "It's five or six miles to town. We will just have to walk it."

Nothing could get Toad out of bed the next morning. So Mole and Rat got to work. Rat saw to the horse and started a fire and cleaned the cups and plates. Mole went to the nearest town for milk and eggs and other things Toad forgot. The two animals were resting by the time Toad woke up.

They had a nice ride that day and camped as before. This time Mole and Rat saw that Toad did his part of work. When the time came to travel next morning, Toad wanted to stay in his bunk, but Rat and Mole pulled him out.

Toad and Water Rat walked behind the cart talking. Well, Toad was talking. Then far behind them they could hear a faint hum, like a faraway bee. Looking back, they saw a small cloud of dust. From the dust a faint “Pop-pop!” cry, like an animal in pain.

The animals went back to talking. Then a gust of wind and a swirl of sound made them jump for the nearest ditch, It was on them! The “Pop-pop” shouted in their ears. They had a look at glass and metal. Then the motor-car, with its driver hugging his wheel, flung a cloud of dust at them.

The old horse had been dreaming as he walked along. The motor-car sent him rearing. He drove the cart back into the deep ditch at the side of the road. It shook, and then it crashed. The yellow cart lay on its side in the ditch.

Rat danced up and down in the road. “You monster!” he shouted, shaking his paws, “You—you—road hogs! I’ll have the law after you!”

Toad sat down in the middle of the dusty road, his legs out before him, and stared at the disappearing motor-car. At times he smiled and said, “Pop-pop!”

Mole tried to help the horse. Then he went to look at the cart on its side in the ditch. It was a sorry sight.

Rat went to help him, but they could not right the cart. “Toad!” they cried. “Come and give us a hand, can’t you!”

The Toad never answered or moved from his seat in the road. They went to see what was the matter with him. They found him with a happy smile on his face. His eyes on the dust of the motor-car. From time to time they could still hear him say “Pop-pop!”